living in new york

living in new york

Alessandra Coppa

Motta Architettura

Edited and published by
24 ORE Cultura srl, Milano

english translation
Sylvia Adrian Notini

cover
Tribeca Loft, Moneo Brock Studio
photo by Michael Moran, New York

First Edition
September 2010

ISBN 978-88-6116-122-1

Abitare a New York

Dopo l'11 settembre

A New York dall'11 settembre 2001 sembra che l'energia abbia cambiato traiettoria, la metropoli pensa meno al denaro e a come farne. Molto è cambiato nella Grande Mela, tuttavia questa città vibra ancora della travolgente e eclettica confluenza di personalità capaci di creare tendenza, cosa che si riflette nella complessità dei suoi interni[1].

Devastata, non solo fisicamente, dall'attentato alle Twin Towers, New York ha saputo infatti reagire e rilanciare il suo carattere costruttivo e irrefrenabile attraverso l'adesione a nuove forme dell'abitare lontani dagli eccessi postmoderni degli anni Ottanta, ma decisamente più etici, e che spaziano dalla cura del dettaglio alla gestione della forma complessiva in cui un alto grado di libertà e di sperimentazione proiettano il progetto domestico nel ri-disegno della città[2].

New York offre oggi un interessante scenario composto da differenti linguaggi e varie soluzioni tipologiche: dalla tradizione tutta americana del loft, a attente ristrutturazioni nei lussuosi palazzi newyorkesi degli anni Venti affacciati su Central Park, da interventi in architetture simbolo del Movimento Moderno, a progetti all'interno di edifici storici anche di tipo non residenziale trasformati in esclusivi condomini.

Lo stimolante confronto tra i diversi progetti mostra una straordinaria varietà materica e compositiva che si inserisce nella ricca e fondamentale tradizione della ricerca architettonica americana sulla casa privata. I progetti presentati sono testimonianza di nuove soluzioni e modi di abitare che tendono in questi ultimi anni a sottolineare il valore dello spazio libero, di luoghi luminosi e aperti, privi di vincoli funzionali e tesi verso nuove qualità urbane e ambientali.

La ricerca dello stile moderno dell'abitare

A New York il cambiamento e la diversità sono la norma e il "manhattanismo", come Rem Koolhaas lo ha definito in *Delirious New York* è la "cultura di congestione" e di inesorabile diversità che la pervade. Il vero spirito dell'architettura di New York risiede nella città stessa, nel suo *genius loci*. La densità, la diversità, la continua alternanza di costruzione e ricostruzione tendono a soffocare i gesti architettonici individuali, domina l'effetto complessivo.

Un concetto essenziale per far luce sulla natura di New York si trova proprio nella densità di sviluppo[3].

Nei tre secoli trascorsi dal primo insediamento europeo sull'isola, nota allora come Nuova Amsterdam, Manhattan è stata mappata, interrata e edificata quasi completamente.

Il luogo è divenuto patrimonio immobiliare o territorio pubblico – edifici privati contro strade, parchi e strutture civiche. La dinamica di proprietà si è estesa verso nord, ma anche, in successive ondate di ricostruzione, verso l'alto, in verticale.

Ancor più di Chicago, New York è stata il luogo di nascita del grattacielo e rimane la città in cui quei palazzi altissimi sono spazi di vita quotidiana per milioni di persone.

Eppure, la rivoluzione strutturale nel XIX secolo non produsse una nuova estetica negli esterni e negli interni. Pur accogliendo prontamente i progressi tecnologici, gli architetti di New York rimasero attaccati agli stili storici e a una ricchezza di decorazioni che si esprimeva in materiali di qualità e in elaborati programmi artistici e scultorei.

Questo fino al termine della Seconda guerra mondiale. Quando l'attività costruttiva riprese, alla fine degli anni Quaranta, tutti i fattori alla base della progettazione erano cambiati: tecnologie, materiali, stile e teoria. I progressi tecnologici come l'impiego dell'acciaio strutturale e della *curtain-wall* resero possibili nuove forme architettoniche. L'aria condizionata e l'illuminazione a fluorescenza liberarono le facciate e le piante degli edifici dalla tradizionale dipendenza dalle finestre mobili, necessarie per la ventilazione, e dai cortili interni ricavati nella massa degli edifici per far penetrare la luce negli ambienti. Queste innovazioni tecniche produssero i cambiamenti più profondi nella cultura dell'abitare a New York.

La casa americana, tradizione, riuso e *gentrification*

La tipologia della casa di abitazione ha conosciuto in America forti tradizioni[4] che si possono riconoscere ancora oggi con nuove figure e soluzioni domestiche in continuo mutamento.

Si tratta di una sinergica commistione compositiva e progettuale tra le tre grandi concezioni dello spazio domestico importate dai coloni europei nei secoli scorsi, che insieme alle successive immigrazioni dall'oriente hanno formato una società multietnica. La prima consiste nella proiezione dello spazio interno verso l'esterno con *bow-window* e ampie vetrate come nella tradizione anglosassone. La seconda è l'attenzione mitteleuropea per gli spazi introversi. La terza tradizione architettonica privilegia invece l'espandersi delle stanze verso il mondo esterno con verande, logge e terrazze come nella tradizione mediterranea[5]. In alcune soluzioni invece permane il concetto di identità tra architettura e arredo, proveniente dal mondo anglosassone, filtrata e rielaborata dagli architetti americani dall'Ottocento ai giorni nostri.

Insieme a questa complessa tradizione progettuale che accoglie differenti linguaggi e soluzioni progettuali, negli interni pubblicati emerge anche la tipologia, tutta newyorkese, del loft, antico deposito urbano trasformato in appartamento open-space.

Attualmente un'attenzione particolare è riservata alla ristruttura-zione, al riuso. Il fenomeno del riuso del manufatto urbano emer-ge, non solo a livello europeo, come uno dei fattori di riferimento del generale sforzo di gestione e riqualificazione della città del nuovo millennio di cui New York è indiscussa protagonista.

Si sta ora investendo sulla ristrutturazione dei vecchi edifici industriali che si stanno trasformando in nuovi quartieri borghesi. Esempi di questa crescente *gentrification* dei quartieri sono i Meatpacking District vicino al fiume Hudson, luogo preferito tra i giovani professionisti della città e la zona di Harlem[6].

La ristrutturazione dei vecchi edifici riconvertiti a scopo residen-ziale è un tema che attraversa gli interessi immobiliari in città in questo momento, insieme alle "brownstone" e agli appartamenti di lusso che si trovano a ovest. Inoltre alcuni appartamenti, ricavati in importanti palazzi residenziali newyorkesi costruiti a cavallo dell'ultimo secolo ai bordi di Central Park, denunciano un ricercato e creativo confronto progettuale con la storia dell'edifi-cio che li accoglie.

Il desiderio dominante è quello di ridisegnare e reinventare appartamenti di tipo tradizionale nell'idea di ottenere ambienti più liberi e meno frammentati, aperti verso la città per sfruttarne l'eccezionale skyline.

Loft

Si accennava alla "tradizione" del loft. Il loft, nell'accezione data a questo termine dall'abitare contemporaneo, è immediata-mente riconducibile alla città di New York, a quando negli anni Sessanta i primi artisti occupavano depositi e magazzini a Soho per stabilirvi i propri studi-abitazione. Da allora è diventata una sorta di tipologia domestica internazionale, un termine impie-gato per indicare un grande spazio unitario, in genere di tipo industriale, che viene riutilizzato per ospitare attività diverse da quelle originarie.

Così se in questi ambienti troviamo ancora studi di pittori e scultori, è facile vedervi anche studi professionali e esclusive abitazioni.

"L'altra causa dell'apparizione dei loft sta nel progressivo abbandono dei vecchi edifici industriali da parte delle impre-se che li occupavano e che a un certo punto hanno preferito trasferirsi in edifici meglio equipaggiati e più competitivi"[7]. È questa la ragione per cui i loft non sono disseminati in tutta la città, ma al contrario, di solito, si concentrano in determinate zone con un passato industriale come Soho, Clerkenwell a Londra o il Poblenou a Barcellona. Dunque, questa nuova tipologia abitativa raccoglie una duplice eredità: "da un lato, lo stile di vita convenzionale degli artisti e l'integrazione in un unico spazio dell'abitazione e dell'ambiente di lavoro; dall'altro lato, un'estetica industriale che si manifesta nelle rifiniture degli edifici"[8]. Il loft, dunque, è uno spazio ampio, quasi sempre riconvertito da un precedente uso non abitativo, e spesso con la struttura e gli impianti a vista. Il loft presenta quella che sarà la caratteristica principale delle abitazioni del futuro: grandi spazi flessibili che possono mutare nel tempo secondo le necessità degli occupanti. Difatti, in architettura appare uno degli esempi più efficaci di riciclaggio e riutilizzazione, due concetti chiave per il XXI secolo.

Tendenze living

I progetti presentati sono testimonianza di nuove soluzioni e modi di abitare che tendono a sottolineare il valore dello "spazio libero", nella configurazione di interni luminosi e aperti, privi di vincoli funzionali e tesi verso nuove qualità ambientali.

L'esame parallelo tra loft, spazi reinventati e appartamenti, evidenzia dei rilevanti slittamenti e delle sinergiche commistioni tra le diverse tipologie, che fino a qualche anno fa rimanevano distinte e correvano su binari autonomi[9].

Ad esempio, oggi il loft è impiegato in senso lato per descrivere anche appartamenti ubicati in torri residenziali, ridisegnati a pianta libera, con un'ottimizzazione dell'impiego della luce naturale proveniente dalle pareti perimetrali finestrate, non più nascoste da muri divisori di camere, corridoi e spazi di servizio, e da quella gerarchia distributiva che caratterizzava negli anni passati il tipico appartamento newyorkese. Rispetto ai loft degli anni trascorsi si nota una più approfondita ricerca della soluzione architettonica d'insieme, nell'attenzione rivolta alla cura del dettaglio, all'invenzione tipologico-compositiva e alle scelte materico-cromatiche.

Così se da una parte il loft diventa un'abitazione caratterizzata da una vasta zona giorno multifunzionale, dall'altra molti degli appartamenti selezionati testimoniano, nella loro varietà compositiva e differenza progettuale, la tendenza ad abbandonare il consueto impianto a stanze separate con corridoio distributivo. Se viene sempre mantenuta la scansione tra zona giorno e notte, garantendo la necessaria privacy di quest'ultima, spesso le tradizionali sala da pranzo e cucina, biblioteca e soggiorno, si uniscono in riuscite commistioni funzionali, all'interno di un unico grande spazio che, proprio per le sue generose dimensioni, ricorda le caratteristiche del loft[10].

Le ultime tendenze più in voga nella progettazione dei nuovi loft, dagli enormi spazi industriali ai piccoli edifici, sfruttano al massimo le possibilità spaziali per creare una sensazione di dilatabilità, mettendo in evidenza le strutture portanti.

Note

[1] A.Taschen, *Ritorno a New York*, in *New York Interiors*, Taschen, Köln 2008, p. 9.

[2] M. Vercelloni, *Urban interiors in New York*, Edizioni L'Archivolto, Milano 1996, pp. 8.

[3] C. Willis, Introduzione, in A. Johnson, *L'architettura di New York*, Rizzoli Skira, New York 2003.

[4] Si veda C. Norberg –Schulz, *L'architettura del Nuovo Mondo, tradizione e sviluppo nell'architettura americana*, Officina Edizioni, 1988, pp. 15-63 e C. W. Moore, K. Smith, P. Becker, *Home sweet home - american domestic vernacular architecture*, Craft and Folk Art Museum Los Angeles, Rizzoli New York, 1983.

[5] M. Vercelloni, *Urban interiors in New York*, Edizioni L'Archivolto, Milano 1996, pp. 8-9.

[6] A. Coppa, *Identità e memorie delle Brownstone ad Harlem*, in S. Pozzoli, *On the block. Harlem private view*, Umberto Allemandi & C. per Montrasio Arte, Torino, 2010, pp. 18-21.

[7] F.A. Cerver, *Vivere in un loft*, Logos, Modena 2004, pp. 6-7; si veda AA.VV., *I loft americani*, in "Lotus International", 66, novembre 1990. Numero interamente dedicato alla tradizione del loft americano, A. Coppa, *Loft e attici d'autore*, Collana Architetture d'autore, Motta Architettura, Milano 2007.

[8] *Ibidem.*

[9] M. Vercelloni, *New York stories*, in *Lofts & Apartments* in NY, Edizioni L'Archivolto, Milano 2006, pp. 8-9.

[10] M. Vercelloni, *Lofts & Apartments* … cit., pp. 8-9.

Alessandra Coppa

Living in New York

After September 11

Since September 11, the energy in New York City seems to have taken a sharp turn. These days, the city spends much less time thinking about money and how to make it. Although a great deal has changed about the Big Apple, the city still vibrates with the overwhelming and open-minded convergence of its trend-setting personalities, and this is reflected in the complexity of its interiors.[1] Devastated, not just physically, by the attack on the Twin Towers, New York was nonetheless capable of reacting and relaunching its constructive, unstoppable temperament by adhering to new forms of living - more ethical ones - far from the Post-Modern excesses of the 1980s. These range from attention to detail to the management of form in general, so that a great degree of freedom and experimentation have turned housing into a way to redesign the city.[2]

The New York architectural scene today is an interesting one, made up of many different languages and a wide variety of typological solutions: from the all-American tradition of the loft, to detailed renovations in the city's deluxe 1920s buildings over-looking Central Park; from architectural interventions symbol-izing the Modern Movement, to projects developed from within historical buildings, some of which originally non-residential, now converted into exclusive condominiums.

The exciting comparison between all of these projects reveals an extraordinary variety of textures and compositions that have found a place for themselves in the interesting and basic tradition of American architectural research into private homes. These projects bear witness to new solutions and new ways of living, which in recent years tend to emphasize the value of free space, of open spaces flooded with light, of places where functional restrictions are non-existent and the tendency is to take urban and environmental qualities into account.

The search for a modern style of living

Change and diversity are the rule in New York, and "Manhattanism", the word used by Rem Koolhaas in *Delirious New York*, is the "culture of congestion" and of inexorable diversity that pervades the city. The soul of New York's architecture resides right there in the city, in its distinctive atmosphere. The density, diversity, and continual alternating between construction and reconstruction tend to stifle individual architectural gestures. What prevails here is the overall effect.

But if we want to understand the city's temperament, we need

to consider its density of development.[3] Over the last three centuries, from the first European settlement on the island of New
Amsterdam, as it was called back then, Manhattan has been
mapped, developed underground and almost totally rebuilt. It is
now entirely made up of either real estate or public land - private
buildings versus streets, parks and civic architecture. Property
dynamics extend northwards, but with one wave of construction
after another, upwards - meaning vertically - as well.

Much more than Chicago, New York is the place where the sky-
scraper was born, and it continues to be the city where very tall
buildings provide space to millions of people as they go about
their lives each day.

And yet the 19th century's structural revolution did not create
a new aesthetic in interior and exterior design. Although they
welcomed technology, New York architects remained faithful to
historical styles and to an abundance of ornamentations made
out of high-quality materials and founded on elaborate artistic
and sculptural programmes.

This lasted until World War II ended. When construction was
resumed in the late 1940s, the principles of architecture - technology, material, style and theory - had changed. Progress in
technology, the use of stainless steel frames and curtain walls,
for instance, signified the development of new architectural
forms. Air conditioning and fluorescent lighting liberated building façades and plans from their traditional dependence on the
openable windows needed to control the passage of air, as well
as from the hollowing out of inner courtyards in the building
block in order to receive light. The most significant changes in
New York's culture of living were based on technical innovations
such as these.

The American home, tradition, adaptive re-use and gentrification

The typology of the American home is founded on very strong
traditions;[4] these are still visible today in the form of new figures
and domestic solutions that are constantly shifting. The synergic
combination of composition and design stems from the three
most important traditions in domestic space, brought over by
Europeans through the centuries, who were later joined by immi-
grants from Eastern countries to form a multiethnic society. The
first of these architectural traditions resides in the outwards pro-
jection of interior space through the use of bow windows or very
large glass panes - a nod to Anglo-Saxon tradition. The second
tradition is based on the Mittel-European concern with intro-
verted spaces. The third tradition fosters the expansion of rooms

towards the exterior through the use of verandas, open-sided extensions and balconies reminiscent of the Mediterranean.[5] Visible in some of the solutions is the notion of the identity between architecture and interior decoration of Anglo-Saxon inspiration, filtered and reworked by American architects from the 19th century to the present.

Alongside this complex tradition in design made up of a number of languages and building solutions is the interior typology known as the loft, typical of New York. These are spaces that were at one time used for storage but have since been transformed into apartments characterized by their adaptable open space.

These days, a great deal of attention is being paid to renovation and re-use. The phenomenon of adaptive re-use in urban architecture - also present in Europe - has become a point of reference for widespread efforts to manage and requalify the city of the new millennium, within which New York plays an undisputed leading role.

The investments currently being made to renovate old industrial buildings are giving rise to new middle-class neighbourhoods. The Meatpacking District close to the Hudson River, which especially caters to the city's young professionals, and Harlem are two examples of the growing gentrification of New York's neighbourhoods.[6]

At present, real estate interests focus on issues concerning the renovation of old buildings to be re-used for housing, brownstones and deluxe apartments on the city's West Side. Moreover, apartments constructed in some of New York's most important turn-of-the-century residential buildings overlooking Central Park offer creative designs that act as a foil to the history of their location.

What prevails is the desire to redesign and reinvent apartments featuring a traditional typology, but aimed at achieving spaces that are freer and less fragmentary, spaces that open out in the direction of the city to exploit the exceptional skyline.

The Loft

But let's go back to the "tradition" of the loft. The "loft", which is the word coined for this type of contemporary housing, first originated in New York in the 1960s when artists began inhabiting storage warehouse spaces in Soho to create their homes and studios. Since then, the loft has become a housing typology worldwide. The word is used to indicate a large, single space, generally of the industrial kind, which is re-used for activities that have nothing to do with the original purpose of the location. Lofts are now used as creative work spaces for painters and sculptors, offices for professionals or simply as homes.

"Another reason why lofts came into being was because of the abandonment of old industrial buildings by the companies that were once located there, when they chose to make an upscale move to buildings that were better equipped and more competitive".[7]

This is why lofts are not spread throughout the city but, on the contrary, quite often concentrated in specific neighbourhoods with an industrial past: Soho in New York, Clerkenwell in London, Poblenou in Barcelona, and so on. This new typology stems from a twofold reality: "on the one hand, what is widely held to be the lifestyle of artists and their use of a single space as a home and work environment; on the other, the industrial aesthetic manifested in the nonstructural parts of the building".[8] The loft is thus a large, open space, nearly always converted from previous non-residential use, and in most cases it adheres to the original look of the building by leaving structural and nonstructural parts exposed. We might add that what is typical of the loft today will be an essential feature of homes in the future: wide, flexible spaces modifiable in time depending on the needs of the occupants. Architecturally speaking, it is one of the most effective examples of two core concepts for the 21st century: recycling and re-use.

Trends in living

The designs presented bear witness to new solutions and new ways of living that tend to emphasize the value of "free space", visible in well-lit, open-spaced interiors, where functional restrictions are non-existent and where new environmental qualities are the trend.

A parallel examination of lofts, reinvented spaces and apartments reveals major shifting in the synergic blending of these different typologies, which up until a few years ago remained distinct and ran along separate tracks.[9]

Today, the word loft is also used to describe residential tower apartments redesigned with a free plan, where every effort is made to exploit the natural light that seeps in through perimeter walls with windows, no longer hidden by walls erected to partition off the rooms, by corridors or by amenity spaces; nor by the distributive hierarchy that once characterized the typical New York apartment. If compared to lofts of the past, what we observe here is an in-depth research into the architectural solution as a whole, evident in the attention to detail, typological-composite scheme, and choice of materials and colours.

In short, if on the one hand the loft becomes a home characterized by a vast multifunctional living area, on the other, because of their differences in composition and design, many of the apartments selected reveal a tendency to abandon the usual separate-rooms-with-main-corridor arrangement. When the distinction between the living and sleeping areas is maintained, guaranteeing the privacy of the latter, the traditional dining room, kitchen, study and living room are often successfully combined for the sake of function into one large space, which, precisely because of its generous dimensions, recalls the features of the loft.[10]

The most recent trends in the newest designs for lofts, from huge industrial spaces to small buildings, fully exploit what is offered in terms of space in order to create a feeling of expandability, at the same time leaving the support structures exposed.

Notes

[1] A. Taschen, "Ritorno a New York," in *New York Interiors* (Köln: Taschen, 2008), p. 9.

[2] M. Vercelloni, *Urban Interiors in New York* (Milan: Edizioni Archivolto, 1996), p. 8.

[3] C. Willis, "Introduction," in *L'architettura di New York* by A. Johnson (New York: Rizzoli Skira, 2003).

[4] See C. Norberg-Schulz, *L'architettura del Nuovo Mondo, tradizione e sviluppo nell'architettura americana* (Rome: Officina Edizioni, 1998), pp. 15-63, and C.W. Moore, K. Smith, P. Becker, *Home Sweet Home: American Domestic Vernacular Architecture* (New York: Rizzoli, 1983); exhibition catalogue for the Los Angeles Craft and Folk Art Museum.

[5] M. Vercelloni, *Urban Interiors in New York* (Milan: Edizioni Archivolto, 1996), pp. 8-9.

[6] A. Coppa, "Identità e memorie delle Brownstone ad Harlem," in *On the Block. Harlem Private View* by S. Pozzoli (Turin: Umberto Allemandi & C. for Montrasio Arte, 2010), pp. 18-21.

[7] F.A. Cerver, *Vivere in un loft* (Modena: Logos, 2004), pp. 6-7; see "I loft americani," *Lotus International*, 66 (November 1990). Issue entirely dedicated to the American loft tradition, A. Coppa, *Loft e attici d'autore* in the Architetture d'autore series (Milan: Motta Architettura, 2007).

[8] *Ibid.*

[9] M. Vercelloni, "New York Stories," in *Lofts & Apartments in New York* (Milan: Edizioni Archivolto, 2006), pp. 8-9.

[10] M. Vercelloni, *Lofts & Apartments in New York*, op. cit., pp. 8-9.

Alessandra Coppa

living in new york

Mercer Street Loft #1

Deborah Berke & Partners Architects

year	1999
address	Mercer Street
photos	Fabien Baron
site	www.dberke.com

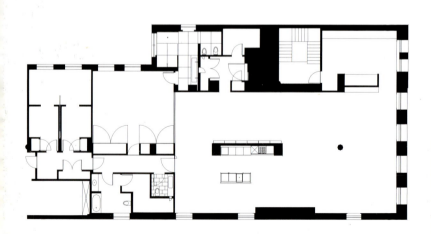

0 1   5m   O

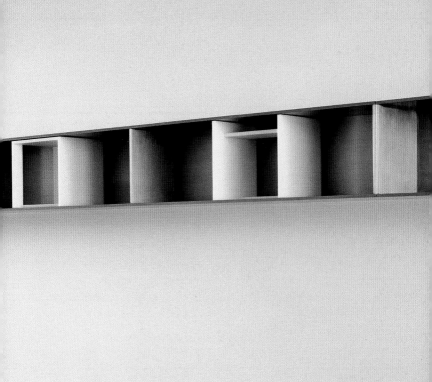

Jay Street Building & Atelier

Deborah Berke & Partners Architects

year	2006
address	Jay Street
photos	Catherine Tighe
site	www.dberke.com

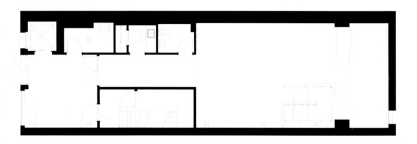

+1

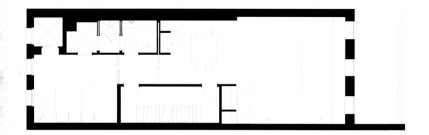

+2

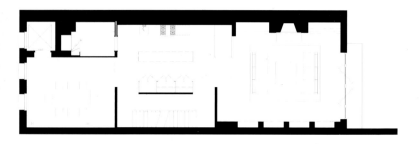

0 1   5m

+3

92 Warren Condos

Chelsea Atelier Architect - Ayhan Ozan

year	2007
address	92 Warren Street
collaborators	Ayhan Ozan (interior architects), Manuel Glas (architect)
photos	Bjorg Magnea
site	www.chelseaatelier.com

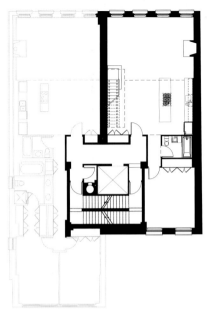

0 1 5m

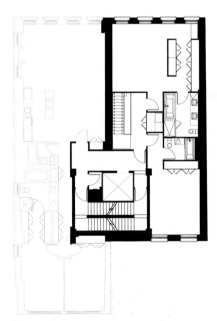

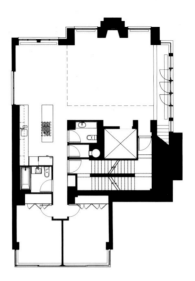

0 1 5m

+12

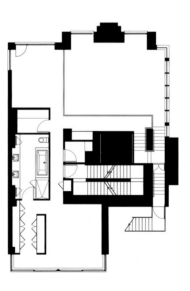

+13

Chelsea Loft

Chelsea Atelier Architect - Ayhan Ozan

year	2009
address	245 7th Avenue
collaborators	Chelsea Atelier Architect: Ayhan Ozan, AIA principal (architect)
photos	Rick Lew
site	www.chelseaatelier.com

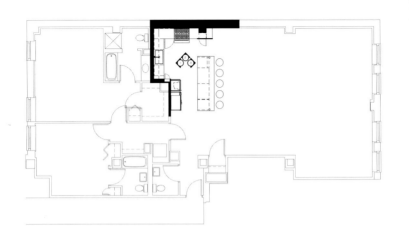

0 1   3m   0

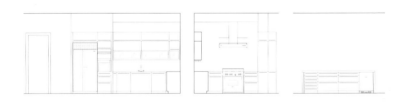

0 1   3m

NY Duplex

Chelsea Atelier Architect - Ayhan Ozan

year	2002
address	221 East 50th Street
collaborators	Ayhan Ozan (architect)
photos	Bjorg Magnea
site	www.chelseaatelier.com

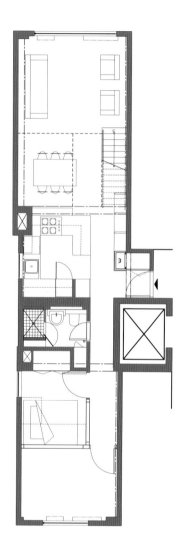

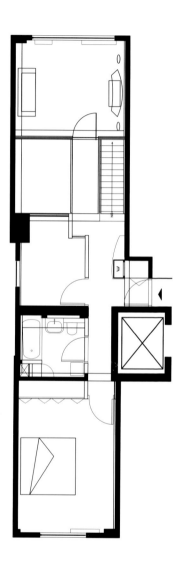

Cooper Square

Desai/Chia Architecture

year	2004
collaborators	Katherine Chia (architect),
	Arjun Desai, Philip Kerzner (project design team)
	Christine Sciulli Light + Design (lighting consultant)
	Attila Rona, P.E., Donald Friedman, P.E. (structural engineers)
	Simon Rodkin Consulting Engineers (mechanical engineer)
photos	Paul Warchol
site	www.desaichia.com

0 1   5m

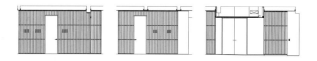

0 1 5m

Flower District Loft

Desai/Chia Architecture

year	2004
collaborators	Cooley Monato Studio (lighting consultant)
	Simon Rodkin Consulting Engineers (mechanical engineer)
photos	Paul Warchol
	Joshua McHugh
site	www.desaichia.com

0 1 5m

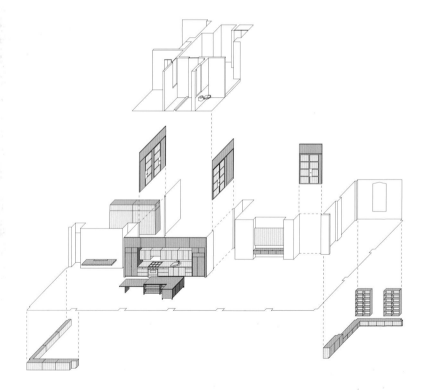

Light_box Loft

Desai/Chia Architecture

year	2007
collaborators	Christine Sciulli Light + Design (lighting consultant)
	Simon Rodkin Consulting Engineers (mechanical engineer)
photos	Paul Warchol
site	www.desaichia.com

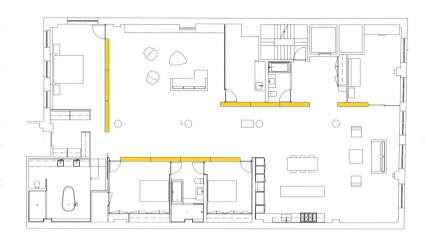

0 1 5m

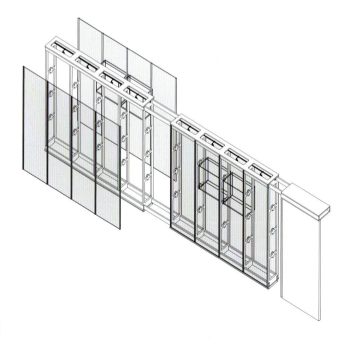

Madison Square

Desai/Chia Architecture

year	2007
collaborators	Christine Sciulli Light + Design (lighting consultant)
	Simon Rodkin Consulting Engineers (mechanical engineer)
photos	Paul Warchol
site	www.desaichia.com

0 1 5m

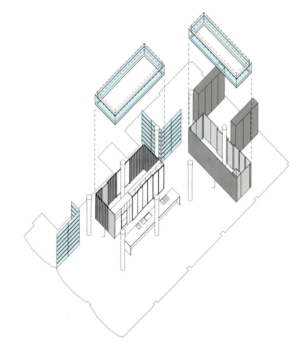

Broadway Loft

Roger Ferris + Partners

year	2001
collaborators	Roger Ferris, Myron Mirgorodsky, Tiziano Fabrizio (design team), Ove Arup & Partners Usa (engineer)
photos	Paul Rivera
site	www.ferrisarch.com

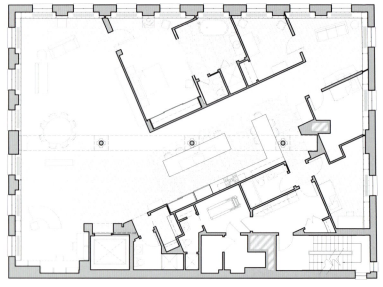

0 1   5m   +1

Gymnasium Apartment

Gwathmey Siegel & Associates Architects

year	2002
address	240 Centre Street
collaborators	Thomas A. Polise Engineers (mechanical engineer),
	Severud Associates (structural engineer)
	Hillmann DiBernardo Leiter & Castelli (lighting designer)
	Cerami & Associates (acoustics consultant)
photos	Paul Warchol
site	www.gwathmey-siegel.com

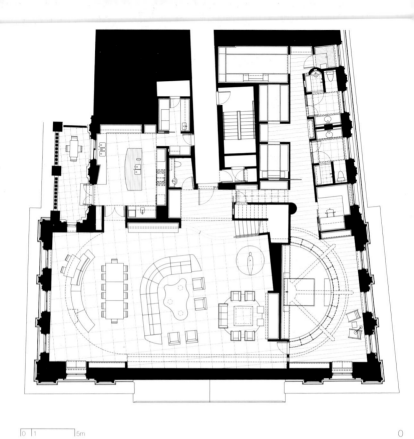

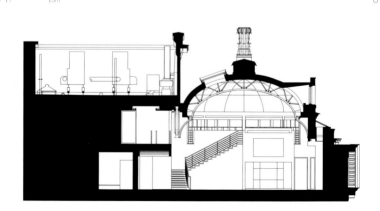

144

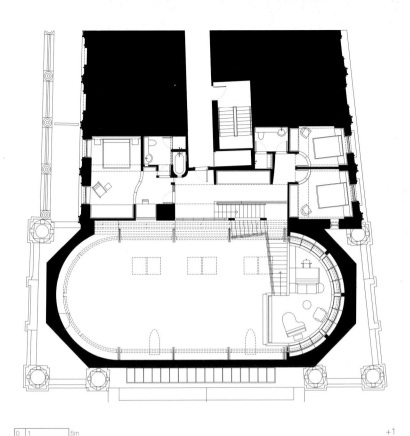

0 | 1 | 5m

+1

147

Carnegie Hill Residence

Hariri & Hariri Architecture

year	2006
address	Park Avenue
collaborators	Gisue Hariri, Mojgan Hariri, Thierry Pfister (design team)
	IP Group Consulting Engineers (MEP engineers)
	DCM Systems (audio-visual consultant)
photos	Paul Warchol
site	www.haririandhariri.com

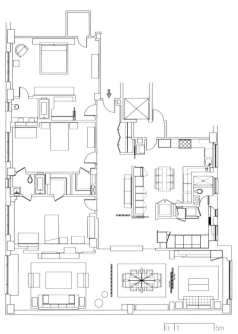

0 1   5m

Fifth Avenue Penthouse

Hariri & Hariri Architecture

year	1998
collaborators	Gisue Hariri, Mojgan Hariri, Karin Mousson (design team), Robert Silman Associates P.C., Joe Tortorella (structural engineer), Szekely Engineering (mechanical engineer)
photos	Paul Warchol
site	www.haririandhariri.com

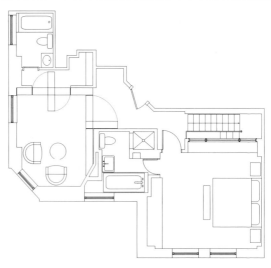

0 1 3m

+21

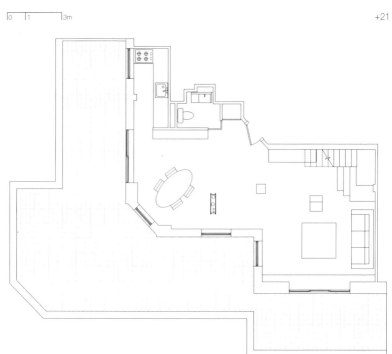

+20

Sutton Place Residence

Hariri & Hariri Architecture

year	2008
address	Sutton Place
collaborators	Gisue Hariri, Mojgan Hariri, Thierry Pfister
	Bieinna Ham (design team)
	IP Group Consulting Engineers (MEP engineers)
	Lighting Workshop (lighting consultant)
	DCM Systems (audio-visual consultant)
photos	Paul Warchol
site	www.haririandhariri.com

0 1   5m

Soho Duplex

David Hotson
Architect

year	2000
address	Greene Street
photos	Eduard Hueber
site	www.hotson.net

0 1   5m

Morgan / Cary Town House

Beyhan Karahan & Associates Architects

year	2007
address	441 West 21st Street
collaborators	Elizabeth Morgan (interior design), Marcy Ramos (HVAC engineering), Severud Associates (structural engineering)
photos	Costa Picadas
site	www.beyhankarahan.com

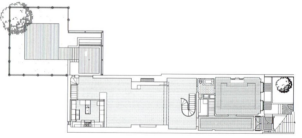

+1

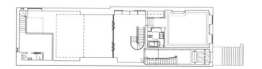

0 1   10m

+2

Private Residence   Paul Latham
Design

year	2008
address	641 5th Avenue
collaborators	Charles Yassky
photos	Costa Picadas
site	www.paullathamdesign.com

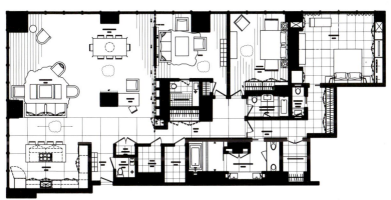

Camera

Diane Lewis
Architect

year	**2007**
address	**Bleeker Street**
photos	**Paul Warchol**

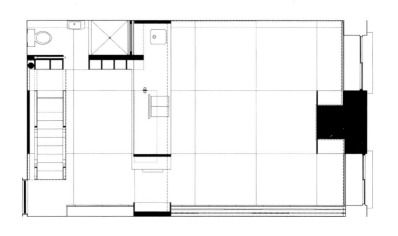

0 1   3m   +1

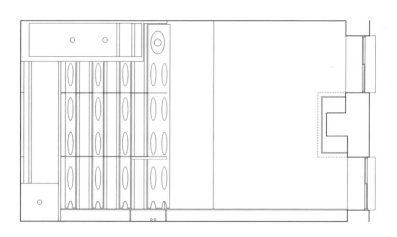

Morton Loft   LOT-EK

year	2000
address	West Village
collaborators	LOT-EK: Ada Tolla, Giuseppe Lignano (principals),
	John Hartmann (project architect)
photos	Paul Warchol
site	www.lot-ek.com

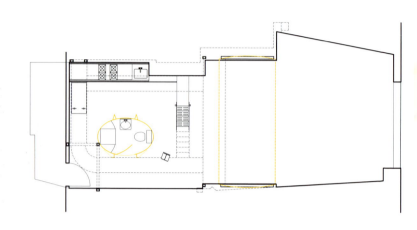

0   1   3m

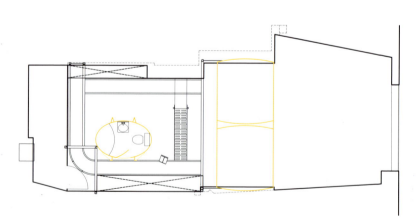

SoHo Studio Loft   Gates Merkulova Architects

year	2008
address	478 West Broadway
collaborators	Paul Gates, Zhenya Merkulova
photos	Michael Moran
site	www.gmarch.com

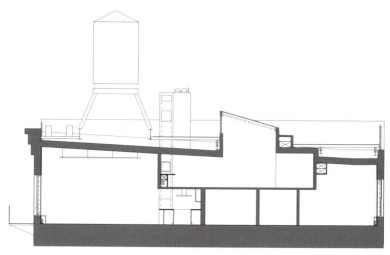

0 1 5m

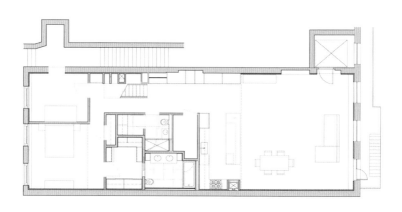

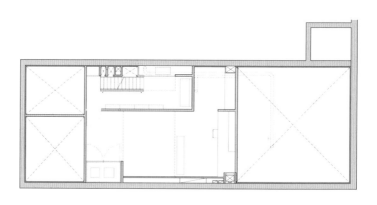

248

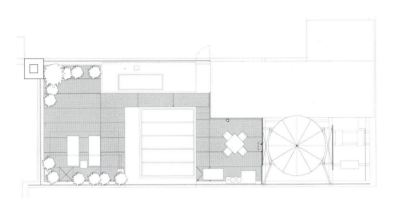

+6

0   1   5m

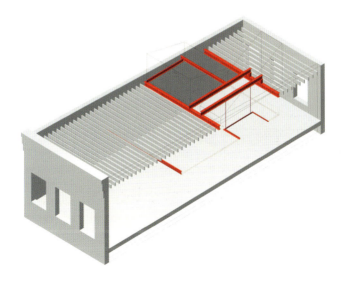

0 1   5m

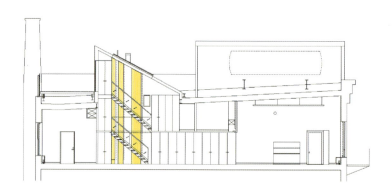

Hudson Loft

Moneo Brock Studio

year	2000
address	Hudson Street
collaborators	Belén Moneo, Jeff Brock, Robert Robinowitz (design architect),
	Belén Moneo (project architect),
	Ryan Enchede, David Griffin, Marcos Velasco (MBS staff)
photos	Michael Moran
site	www.moneobrock.com

0 | 1 | 5m

Tribeca Loft

Moneo Brock Studio

year	1994
address	Varick Street
collaborators	Belén Moneo, Jeff Brock (design architect),
	Belén Moneo (project architect)
photos	Michael Moran
site	www.moneobrock.com

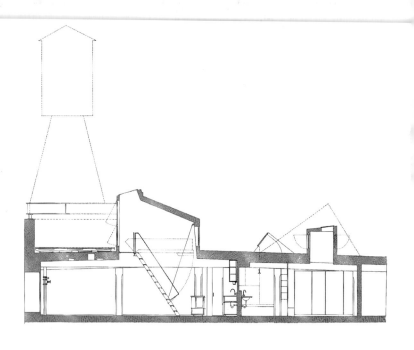

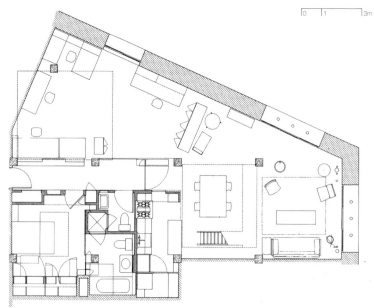

81 Wooster Street   Valerie Pasquiou Interiors+Design

year	2007
address	81 Wooster Street
collaborators	Valerie Pasquiou (interior design)
photos	Costa Picadas
site	www.vpinteriors.com

Hill Loft

Resolution:
4 Architecture

year	1999
address	Tribeca
collaborators	Joseph Tanney, Robert Luntz (architects),
	Catarina Ferreira (project architect)
photos	Eduard Hueber
site	www.re4a.com

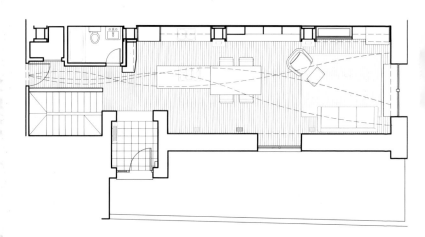

0 1 3m

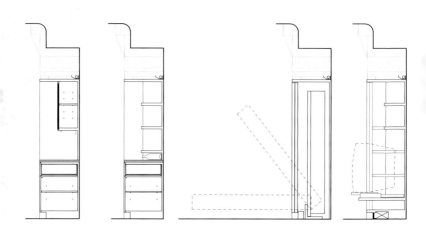

0 1 3m

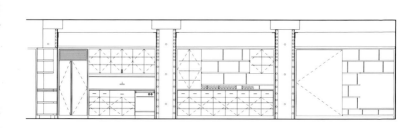

Loft
of Frank & Amy

Resolution:
4 Architecture

year	2000
address	Hell's Kitchen
collaborators	Joseph Tanney, Robert Luntz (architects),
	Daniel Piselli (project architect),
	Michael Anderson, Erin Vali (project team)
photos	Paul Warchol
site	www.re4a.com

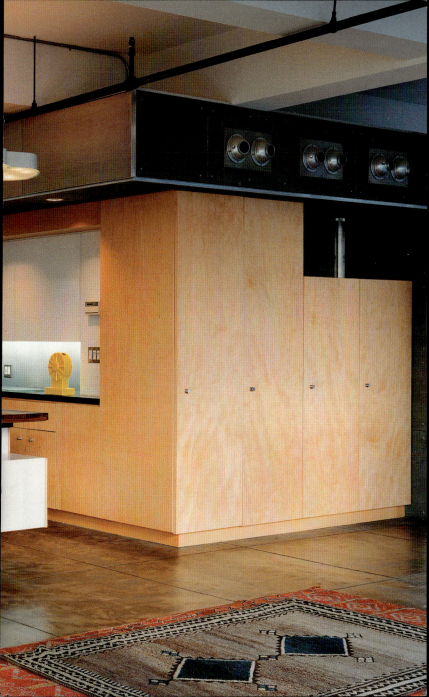

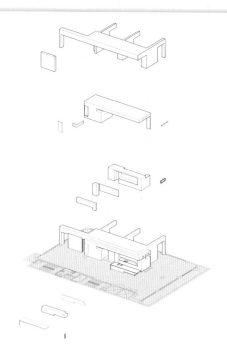

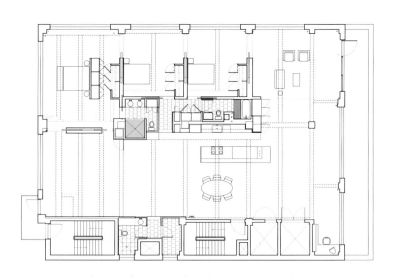

Nychay Loft

Resolution:
4 Architecture

year	2004
address	Soho
collaborators	Joseph Tanney, Robert Luntz (architects),
	Jerome Engelking (project architect),
	Shawn Brown, Mike McDonald (project team)
photos	Floto+Warner
site	www.re4a.com

0 1   5m

Pineapple Loft

Resolution:
4 Architecture

year	2003
address	Brooklyn Heights
collaborators	Joseph Tanney, Robert Luntz (architects)
photos	Res4
site	www.re4a.com

0 1   5m

Potters Pad of Planes

Resolution: 4 Architecture

year	**1997**
address	**Chelsea**
collaborators	**Joseph Tanney, Robert Luntz (architects),**
	Erin Vali, John DaCruz (project architects)
photos	**Eduard Hueber**
site	**www.re4a.com**

0 1   5m

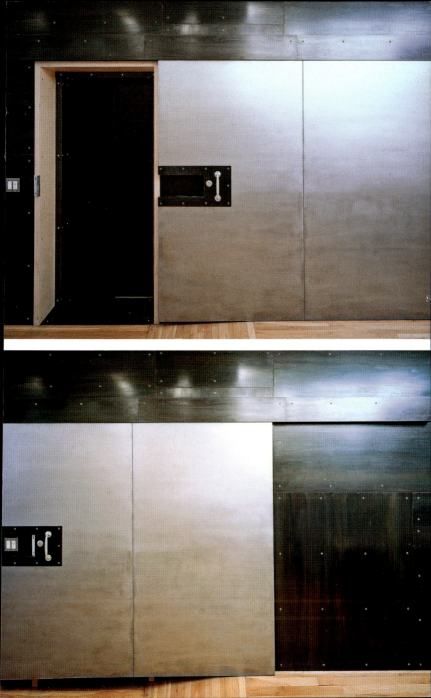

520 West Chelsea   Selldorf Architects

year	2008
address	516 West 19th Street
collaborators	SLCE Architects (architects of record),
	I.M. Robbins & Associates (mechanical/electrical engineers),
	DeSimone Consulting Engineers (structural engineers)
photos	Nikolas Koenig
	Hypertecture Inc. (renders)
site	www.selldorf.com

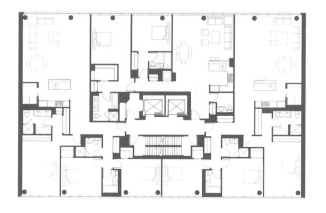

0 1   10m   +3-9

400 West Street

Sixx Design - Robert and Cortney Novogratz

year	2009
address	400 West Street
collaborators	Robert and Cortney Novogratz, Richard Woods
photos	Costa Picadas
site	www.sixxdesign.com

Loft Residence

Shelton, Mindel & Associates

year	1994
photos	Michael Moran
site	www.sheltonmindel.com

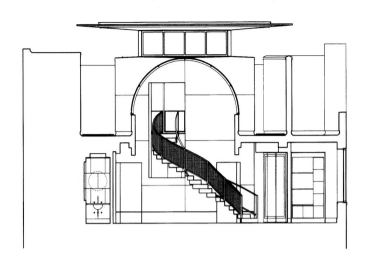

0 1   10m

 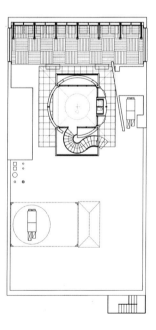

One York

Ten Arquitectos - Enrique Norten

year	2008
address	One York Street
collaborators	Enrique Norten, Tim Dumbleton, Florian Oberhuber, Irina Verona, Javier Pérez-Gil, Pedro Hernandez, Tina Wallbaum, Eugene Sun, Katalina Arboleda, Christopher Glass, Chantal Aquilina, Michael Anisko, Nandini Bagchee, Suzanne Gehlert, Michel Hsiung, Yun Hsueh, Alex Miller, Hyung Seung Min, Ted Wagner, Aida Estebanez
photos	Eduard Hueber
	dbox (renders)
site	www.ten-arquitectos.com

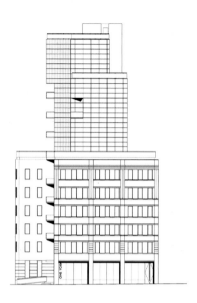

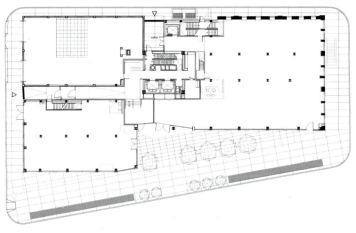

0 1   10m   0

0 1   10m

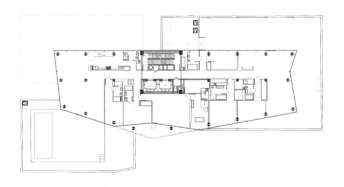

0 1   10m   +7

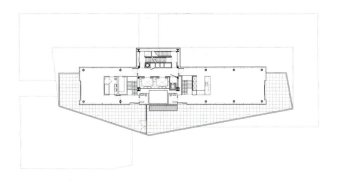

0|1   10m

Alessandra Coppa
Architetto e giornalista
pubblicista, ha conseguito
il dottorato di ricerca
in Storia dell'Architettura
e dell'Urbanistica presso
il Politecnico di Torino
ed è docente di Storia
dell'architettura contemporanea
al Politecnico di Milano.
Collabora per le riviste di
architettura del Gruppo Il Sole
24 ORE. Ha pubblicato per
la collana Minimum (Motta
Architettura, 24 ORE Cultura
le monografie *Mario Botta*
e *Vittorio Gregotti*. Di recente
ha curato la mostra *Zaha Hadid*,
tenutasi presso il Palazzo della
Ragione di Padova (catalogo
Electa, Milano).

Alessandra Coppa
Architect and freelance
journalist, she was awarded
a doctorate in History of
Architecture and Urban Studies
at the Polytechnic of Turin,
and currently teaches History
of Contemporary Architecture
at the Polytechnic of Milan.
She contributes to architecture
journals published by Gruppo
Il Sole 24 ORE. Her publications
include the monographs Mario
Botta *and* Vittorio Gregotti *for*
the Minimum series (published
by Motta Architettura, 24 ORE
Cultura). She recently curated
the Zaha Hadid *exhibition held*
at the Palazzo della Ragione in
Padua (exhibition catalogue by
Electa, Milan).

Printed in Italy
by 24 ORE Cultura, Milan
September 2010